JUSTIN JEFFERSON

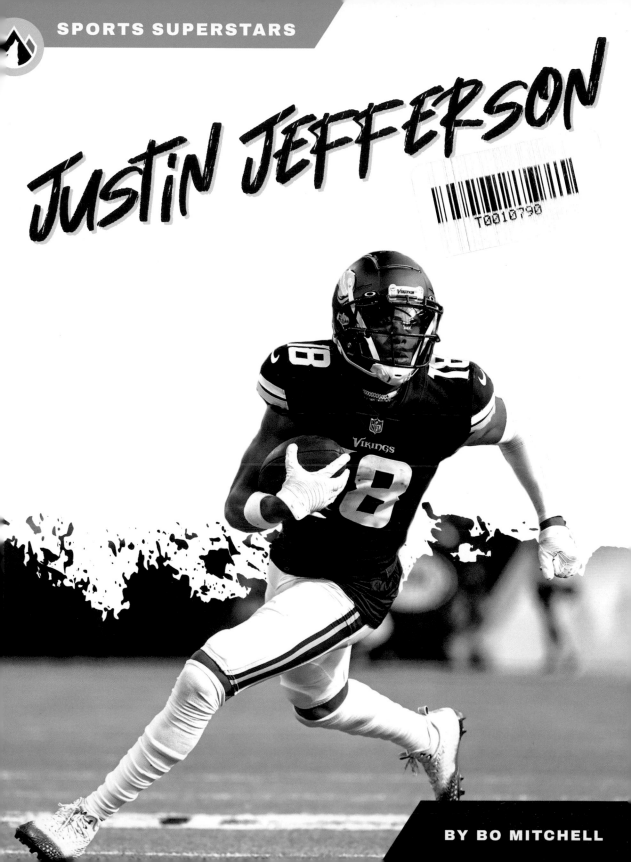

BY BO MITCHELL

Apex is distributed by North Star Editions:
sales@northstareditions.com | 888-417-0195

Produced for Apex by Red Line Editorial.

Photographs ©: Abbie Parr/AP Images, cover; Nick Wosika/SPTSW/AP Images, 1, 26–27; David Stluka/AP Images, 4–5, 6–7, 18–19; Elizabeth Flores/Star Tribune/AP Images, 8–9; Shutterstock Images, 10–11, 12, 16–17; Ross D. Franklin/AP Images, 13, 29; Perry Knotts/AP Images, 14; Brett Duke/AP Images, 20–21; Gregory Bull/AP Images, 22–23; Nick Wass/AP Images, 24

Library of Congress Control Number: 2022922222

ISBN
978-1-63738-556-2 (hardcover)
978-1-63738-610-1 (paperback)
978-1-63738-714-6 (ebook pdf)
978-1-63738-664-4 (hosted ebook)

Printed in the United States of America
Mankato, MN
082023

NOTE TO PARENTS AND EDUCATORS

Apex books are designed to build literacy skills in striving readers. Exciting, high-interest content attracts and holds readers' attention. The text is carefully leveled to allow students to achieve success quickly. Additional features, such as bolded glossary words for difficult terms, help build comprehension.

TABLE OF CONTENTS

CHAPTER 1

TOUCHDOWN DANCE

t's the third week of the 2020 NFL season. The Minnesota Vikings face the Tennessee Titans. Justin Jefferson takes the field for his first game as a **starter**.

The Minnesota Vikings played the Tennessee Titans on September 27, 2020.

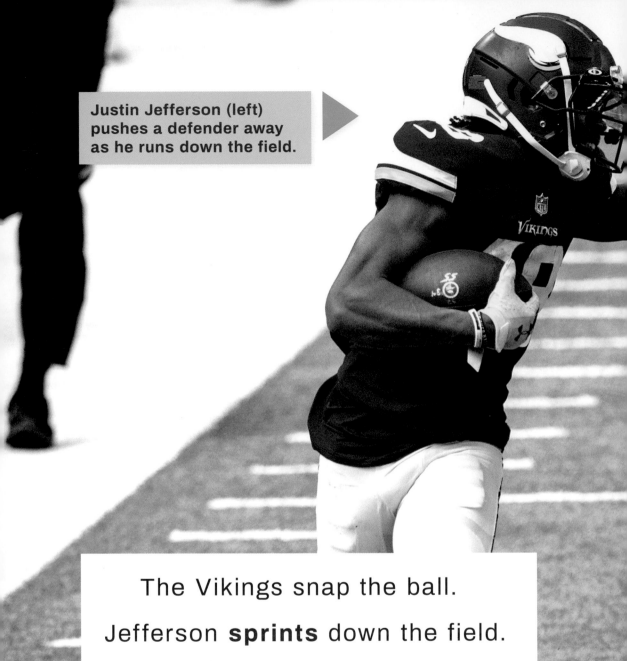

Justin Jefferson (left) pushes a defender away as he runs down the field.

The Vikings snap the ball. Jefferson **sprints** down the field. The quarterback throws the football. Jefferson catches it.

FAST FACT

Jefferson became a starter in his third game with the Vikings. He had seven catches for 175 yards.

Jefferson celebrates as he runs into the end zone.

Jefferson dodges two defenders. He dances into the **end zone**. The fans roar! It's his first NFL touchdown.

THE GRIDDY

In college, Jefferson started doing a dance called the Griddy when he scored. People all over began to copy it. The dance even appeared in video games.

CHAPTER 2

EARLY LIFE

Justin Jefferson grew up in St. Rose, Louisiana. He played **wide receiver** for his high school football team. Justin was a good player. But few colleges tried to **recruit** him.

St. Rose is near New Orleans, which is the largest city in Louisiana.

Justin went to Louisiana State University (LSU). He didn't play much during his first year. But the next year, he had 54 catches and 6 touchdowns.

LSU plays at Tiger Stadium in Baton Rouge, Louisiana.

Justin Jefferson makes a touchdown catch.

ROLE MODELS

Justin has two older brothers. Their names are Jordan and Rickey. Both of them also played football at LSU. Justin looked up to them.

Jefferson's third year was even better. He helped LSU win every game they played that season. They even won the **national championship**.

FAST FACT

In 2019, Jefferson broke the LSU record for most catches in a season.

Jefferson runs down the field during the national championship game.

CHAPTER 3

GOING PRO

After three seasons, Jefferson left LSU to join the NFL. The Minnesota Vikings chose him in the first round of the 2020 **draft**.

The Vikings play at US Bank Stadium in Minneapolis, Minnesota.

Jefferson quickly became an exciting player. He could jump high to make difficult catches. And his speed made him hard to tackle.

FAST FACT

Jefferson's nickname is "Jets." He got this name at LSU because he was so fast.

Jefferson sprints down the field during his first season with the Vikings.

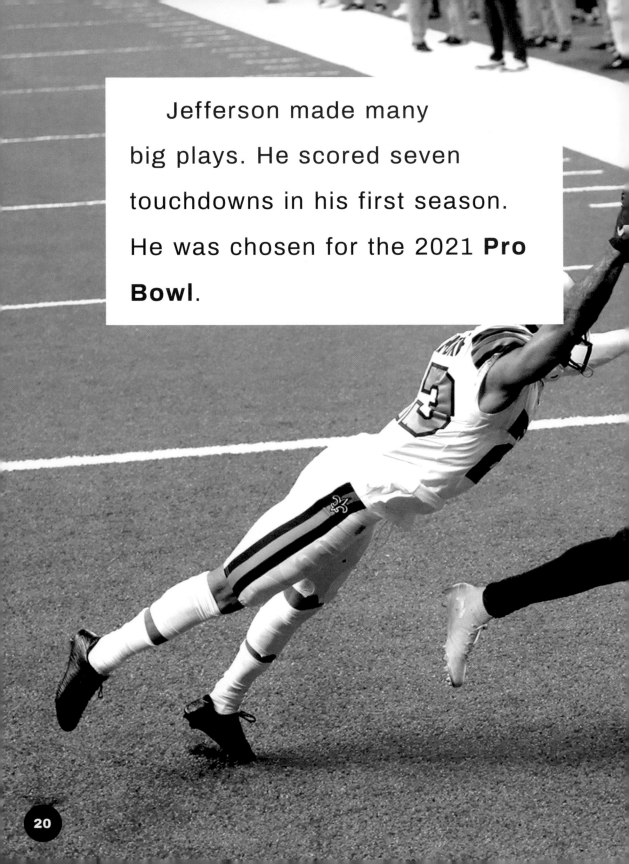

Jefferson made many big plays. He scored seven touchdowns in his first season. He was chosen for the 2021 **Pro Bowl**.

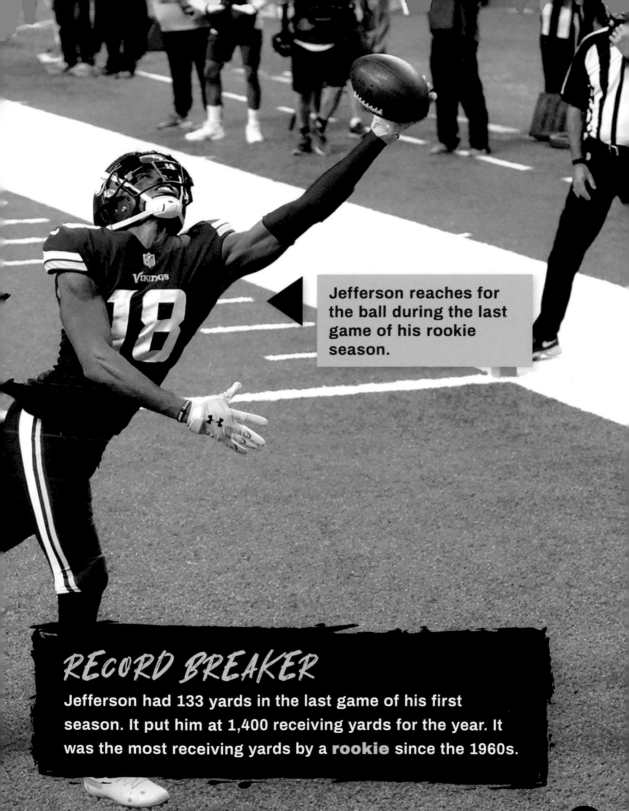

Jefferson reaches for the ball during the last game of his rookie season.

RECORD BREAKER

Jefferson had 133 yards in the last game of his first season. It put him at 1,400 receiving yards for the year. It was the most receiving yards by a **rookie** since the 1960s.

CHAPTER 4

BECOMING A SUPERSTAR

Jefferson was even better in his second season. He had 1,616 receiving yards and 10 touchdowns in 2021.

Jefferson makes a difficult catch in a game against the
Los Angeles Chargers.

Jefferson always kept his eyes on the ball. Other teams could not stop him.

FRIENDLY RIVALS

Jefferson and Ja'Marr Chase were teammates at LSU. Chase joined the NFL in 2021. He played for the Cincinnati Bengals. Chase broke some of Jefferson's records. But the two players stayed close friends.

◀ Jefferson catches a pass during a 2021 game against the Baltimore Ravens.

In 2022, Jefferson was named Offensive Player of the Year.

His 2022 season was historic. He set Vikings records with 128 catches and 1,809 yards. Fans looked forward to more great plays in the future.

FAST FACT

Jefferson made 196 catches in his first two seasons. That tied for the most in NFL history.

COMPREHENSION QUESTIONS

Write your answers on a separate piece of paper.

1. Write a few sentences describing some of the records Justin Jefferson set.

2. Jefferson often does the Griddy after scoring touchdowns. How would you celebrate if you scored a touchdown?

3. Which NFL team drafted Justin Jefferson?

    A. Cincinnati Bengals
    B. Minnesota Vikings
    C. Tennessee Titans

4. Why would jumping high make Jefferson an exciting player?

    A. High jumps help him catch more passes.
    B. High jumps help him make more tackles.
    C. High jumps help him block other players.

5. What does **record** mean in this book?

*In 2019, Jefferson broke the LSU **record** for most catches in a season.*

    A. the best team in the NFL

    B. the worst player on a team

    C. the best or fastest performance

6. What does **historic** mean in this book?

*His 2022 season was **historic**. He set Vikings records with 128 catches and 1,809 yards.*

    A. full of success

    B. slow and steady

    C. hard to explain

Answer key on page 32.

GLOSSARY

draft
A system where professional teams choose new players.

end zone
The end of a football field where teams score touchdowns.

national championship
The final game that decides the best team in college football.

Pro Bowl
A game played after each NFL season involving the best players from each team.

recruit
To get someone to become part of a team or a school.

rookie
A player in their first year.

sprints
Runs very fast for a short period of time.

starter
The best athlete of each position on a team.

wide receiver
A position in football that involves catching passes.

TO LEARN MORE

BOOKS

Coleman, Ted. *Minnesota Vikings All-Time Greats*. Mendota Heights, MN: Press Box Books, 2022.

Halprin, David. *Football Biographies for Kids: The Greatest NFL Players from the 1960s to Today*. Oakland, CA: Rockridge Press, 2022.

Mitchell, Bo. *The Super Bowl*. Mendota Heights, MN: Apex Editions, 2023.

ONLINE RESOURCES

Visit **www.apexeditions.com** to find links and resources related to this title.

ABOUT THE AUTHOR

Bo Mitchell has been writing about sports since the 1990s. He enjoys exercise, music, and having fun with his dog, Rocky. Bo has lived in Minnesota his entire life. He's watched a lot of Minnesota Vikings games.

INDEX

ANSWER KEY:
1. Answers will vary; 2. Answers will vary; 3. B; 4. A; 5. C; 6. A

SABRINA IONESCU

BY ETHAN OLSON

Apex is distributed by North Star Editions:
sales@northstareditions.com | 888-417-0195

Produced for Apex by Red Line Editorial.

Photographs ©: Melissa Tamez/Icon Sportswire/AP Images, cover; Mingo Anthony Nesmith/ Icon Sportswire/AP Images, 1, 4–5, 22–23, 26–27; Erica Denhoff/Icon Sportswire/AP Images, 6; Nam Y. Huh/AP Images, 8–9; Shutterstock Images, 10–11, 16–17, 21, 29; Rich Graessle/Icon Sportswire/AP Images, 12–13; Matt Marton/AP Images, 15; Charlie Litchfield/AP Images, 18–19; John Raoux/AP Images, 20; Noah K. Murray/AP Images, 24

Library of Congress Control Number: 2023901342

ISBN
978-1-63738-555-5 (hardcover)
978-1-63738-609-5 (paperback)
978-1-63738-713-9 (ebook pdf)
978-1-63738-663-7 (hosted ebook)

Printed in the United States of America
Mankato, MN
082023

NOTE TO PARENTS AND EDUCATORS

Apex books are designed to build literacy skills in striving readers. Exciting, high-interest content attracts and holds readers' attention. The text is carefully leveled to allow students to achieve success quickly. Additional features, such as bolded glossary words for difficult terms, help build comprehension.

TABLE OF CONTENTS

CHAPTER 1

YOUNG STAR

The New York Liberty are playing the Minnesota Lynx on May 18, 2021. The Liberty are seven points ahead. But there are five minutes left. And the Lynx have the ball.

Sabrina Ionescu plays point guard for the New York Liberty.

A Lynx player takes a shot. The ball bounces off the rim. Sabrina Ionescu grabs the **rebound**. Then she dribbles down the court.

RECORD SETTER

Ionescu's rebound gave her a triple-double. She became the youngest player in WNBA history to get one. A triple-double is when a player has double digits in three categories. The categories are usually points, **assists**, and rebounds.

Players can also get triple-doubles using categories such as steals or blocks.

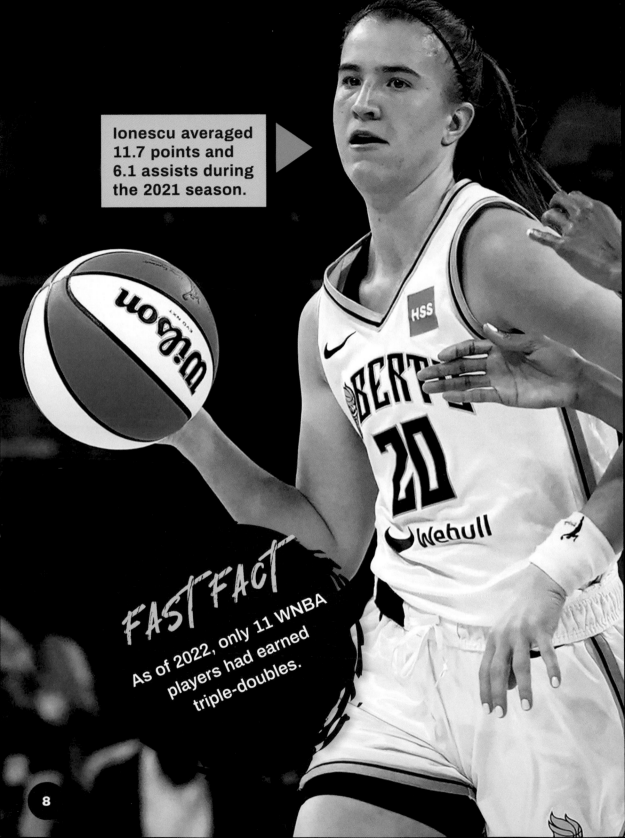

Ionescu averaged 11.7 points and 6.1 assists during the 2021 season.

FAST FACT

As of 2022, only 11 WNBA players had earned triple-doubles.

Later, Ionescu drains a three-pointer. Her teammates cheer. The shot gives the Liberty an even bigger lead. They win the game.

CHAPTER 2

EARLY LIFE

Sabrina Ionescu was born in Walnut Creek, California. Growing up, she loved to play basketball with her twin brother.

Walnut Creek, California, is near San Francisco.

Sabrina played in the 2016 Jordan Brand All-American Classic. It is a game for all-star high school players.

Sabrina often played against boys and older players. But they rarely passed her the ball. So, she focused on rebounding and getting open.

FAST FACT

Sabrina's middle school did not have a girls' basketball team. She found people to start one.

By high school, Sabrina was a great all-around player. She could score, pass, and **defend**. She led her team to the state **championship** in her senior season.

SWEET STATS

Ionescu scored an average of 25.9 points per game during her last year of high school. Her team lost only one game that year. They won 32.

Sabrina was named All-USA Girls Basketball Player of the Year after her senior year.

CHAPTER 3

COLLEGE ICON

Many colleges wanted Sabrina Ionescu to play for them. She chose to attend the University of Oregon.

University of Oregon basketball teams play at Matthew Knight Arena in Eugene, Oregon.

Ionescu was named the PAC-12 Women's Basketball Player of the Year in 2018.

Ionescu dominated in college. No one could stop her from making plays. By her second season, Ionescu led her **conference** in points and assists.

FAST FACT

Ionescu helped Oregon win its conference championship three years in a row.

Ionescu (right) jumps to take a shot during the 2019 Final Four.

Her third year was even better. She helped her team reach the NCAA **playoffs**. They made it all the way to the **Final Four**. Oregon won many games during her senior year, too.

BEST EVER

Ionescu was one of Oregon's best players ever. She scored 26 triple-doubles while on the team. That set an all-time record for the NCAA. Ionescu also won many awards.

The NCAA basketball playoffs are sometimes called March Madness.

CHAPTER 4

GOING PRO

After four years in college, Ionescu was ready to go pro. She entered the 2020 WNBA **Draft**. The New York Liberty chose her.

The New York Liberty used the first pick in the 2020 WNBA Draft to select Ionescu.

Ionescu's first year in the WNBA was rough. She was often injured. But she worked hard to come back. By 2021, she was setting records again.

FAST FACT

The Liberty made the playoffs in 2021. Ionescu scored 14 points in her first playoff game.

Ionescu shoots against the Seattle Storm. The Liberty won 12 out of 32 games in 2021.

Ionescu's great play during the 2022 season earned her a spot on the WNBA All-Star team.

HISTORY MAKER

In 2022, Ionescu got her third triple-double. She had 31 points, 13 rebounds, and 10 assists. No WNBA player had scored more than 30 points in a triple-double game before.

In 2022, Ionescu started every game for the Liberty. She became the team's leading scorer. Fans couldn't wait to see what she did next.

COMPREHENSION QUESTIONS

Write your answers on a separate piece of paper.

1. Write a few sentences describing the main ideas of Chapter 2.

2. If you played basketball, would you focus on scoring, passing, or defending? Why?

3. Which WNBA team drafted Sabrina Ionescu?

   A. Seattle Storm
   B. New York Liberty
   C. Minnesota Lynx

4. What made Ionescu a great all-around player?

   A. She focused on scoring.
   B. She focused on defense.
   C. She focused on every part of the game.

5. What does **dominated** mean in this book?

*Ionescu **dominated** in college. No one could stop her from making plays.*

    A. made a lot of mistakes
    B. had a hard time winning
    C. played very well

6. What does **rough** mean in this book?

*Ionescu's first year in the WNBA was **rough**. She was often injured.*

    A. fast and easy
    B. full of problems
    C. full of success

Answer key on page 32.

GLOSSARY

assists
Times when a player makes a pass that lets another player make a basket.

championship
The final game that decides the winner of a tournament.

conference
A smaller group of teams within a sports league.

defend
To try to stop the other team from scoring.

draft
A system where professional teams choose new players.

Final Four
The last four teams in the NCAA men's or women's college basketball tournament.

playoffs
A set of games played after the regular season to decide which team will be the champion.

rebound
When a player catches the ball after a missed shot.

BOOKS

Buckey, A. W. *Women in Basketball*. Lake Elmo, MN: Focus Readers, 2020.

Omoth, Tyler. *The WNBA Finals*. North Mankato, MN: Capstone Press, 2020.

Sabelko, Rebecca. *Diana Taurasi*. Minneapolis: Bellwether Media, 2023.

ONLINE RESOURCES

Visit **www.apexeditions.com** to find links and resources related to this title.

ABOUT THE AUTHOR

Ethan Olson is a sportswriter based in Minneapolis, Minnesota. He is dedicated to sports but also enjoys making music and exploring nature in his free time. He'd love to cover a World Cup one day.

INDEX

ANSWER KEY:
1. Answers will vary; 2. Answers will vary; 3. B; 4. C; 5. C; 6. B